B
10/18

COMPUTERS

ADVENTURES IN
STEAM

Claudia Martin

Fact Finders®

CAPSTONE PRESS
a capstone imprint

Fact Finders Books are published by Capstone Press,
1710 Roe Crest Drive, North Mankato, Minnesota 56003
www.mycapstone.com

LIBRARY OF CONGRESS CATALOGING-IN-PUBLICATION DATA
Library of Congress Cataloging-in-Publication data is available on the Library of Congress website.
978-1-5435-3229-6 (library binding)
978-1-5435-3324-8 (paperback)
978-1-5435-3551-8 (eBook PDF)

Summary: Closely ties the design, engineering, and programming of computers to the STEAM Initiative. By exploring the ins and outs of these incredible machines, *Computers* offers a deeper understanding of how they work.

EDITORIAL CREDITS
Series editor: Izzi Howell
Designer: Rocket Design (East Anglia) Ltd
Illustrations: Rocket Design (East Anglia) Ltd
In-house editor: Julia Bird

PHOTO CREDITS
Alamy: Mark Scheuern 7b, IanDagnall Computing 22b, Interfoto 30t, ITAR-TASS Photo Agency 30b; Shutterstock: SiiKA Photo 1, luskiv 3 and 29b, goodluz 4, 300 librarians 5, catshila 6, Everett Historical 7t and 23b, MO_SES Premium 9t, Syda Productions 9b, Titima Ongkantong 10, kiri11 11, pinkomelet 12, Parinya Suwannagood 13, Vitaly Korovin 14, MrGarry 15, Tatsianama 16t, Dmitry Kalinovsky 16b, Alexander Kirch 18t, Sudowoodo19, Melody Smart 21, Tim Jenner 22t, Guy Erwood 23c, Oceans 24, Lifestyle Graphic 25t, Lifestyle Graphic 25b, dmitriylo 26, Denis Simonov 27t, N Azlin Sha 27b, MicroOne 28, Barone Firenze 29t, Bloomicon 31c, Peppinuzzo 31b, Ekaphon Maneechot 32, drserg 34, GLYPHstock 35, Wachiwit 36, Oleg Doroshin 38, Zoltan Kiraly 40b, Benny Marty 41b, Veselin Borishev 42, Vidoslava 43, Ahmet Misirligul 45; Wikimedia Commons: Greg Hume 18b, US National Archives and Records Administration 23t, Bcos47 31t, US Navy photo by Chief Photographer's Mate Chris Desmond 37, ESO 40t, NASA/JPL 41, Sunzi99 41c.

Scratch is developed by the Lifelong Kindergarten Group at the MIT Media Lab. See http://scratch. mit.edu. The third party trademarks used in this book are the property of their respective owners, including the Scratch name and logo. The owners of these trademarks have not endorsed, authorized, or sponsored this book.

All design elements from Shutterstock.

First published in Great Britain in 2017 by Wayland

ina at WKT Company Ltd.

TABLE OF CONTENTS

A COMPUTER IS ...

A COMPUTER IS A MACHINE CONTROLLED BY A SET OF INSTRUCTIONS CALLED A PROGRAM. MOST PEOPLE USE COMPUTERS EVERY DAY TO DO ALL SORTS OF THINGS, FROM HELPING WITH HOMEWORK TO LISTENING TO MUSIC.

Computers work with information known as **data**. Computers are able to store data and carry out tasks with it, which is called **processing**. Then computers show the user the results of their work. Modern computers work with data in many different forms, including the following:

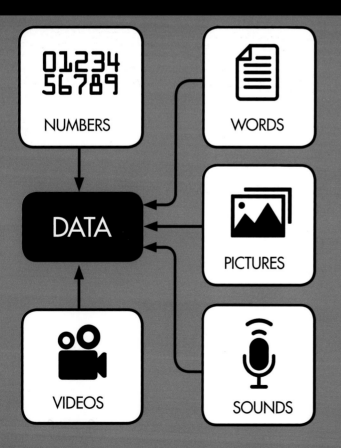

NUMBERS

WORDS

DATA

PICTURES

VIDEOS

SOUNDS

TECHNOLOGY TALK

A program is a list of instructions that tells a computer exactly what work to do. Without programs, computers could not do anything at all. Programs are written by people called computer programmers, or coders. Programs break down any task into its most basic details, telling the computer what to do, step by step. Different programs do different jobs, such as sending emails or playing music.

Software is all the programs that tell a computer what to do. Software is stored and runs on a computer's hardware.

Hardware is all the parts of a computer you can touch. When you look at the computer on your desk, the most obvious pieces of hardware are the screen and keyboard. However, many other bits of hardware are hidden away inside a computer.

Inside a computer, the **motherboard** holds crucial parts. One of these is the **central processing unit (CPU)**, which carries out all the computer's calculations. There are also two types of memory, **RAM** and **ROM** (see page 14), for storing data and programs.

SCIENCE TALK

Today's computers are powered by electricity. The electric currents are small charges of electricity that carry computer data. A desktop computer is plugged into the main electricity supply. Smartphones and laptops are powered by batteries, which can store a certain amount of electrical energy. They need recharging from the main electricity supply.

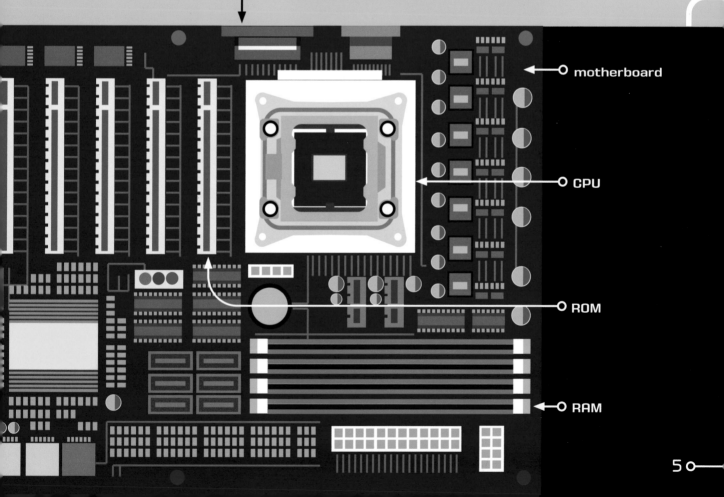

motherboard

CPU

ROM

RAM

IN THE BEGINNING

THOUSANDS OF YEARS AGO, PEOPLE INVENTED CALCULATING DEVICES TO HELP THEM DO MATH. THESE WERE NOT ELECTRONIC MACHINES LIKE TODAY'S COMPUTERS, BUT THEY WERE THE FIRST STEP IN THAT DIRECTION. THE WORD *COMPUTER* WAS FIRST USED IN 1613 TO DESCRIBE A PERSON WHO DID CALCULATIONS.

The abacus appeared over 4,000 years ago. Like modern calculators, the abacus was a machine that performed math operations by simplifying them. It was a step up from using stones or a tally chart to help with counting. The Chinese-style abacus has several rods. In the upper section of each rod, there are two beads. In the lower section, there are five beads.

- On the first rod on the right, the upper beads represent fives, while the lower beads represent ones.

- On the second rod from the right, the upper beads represent fifties and the lower beads represent tens.

- The values continue to increase by a factor of 10—to hundreds, thousands, and so on.

PROJECT

If you have an abacus or can make a basic one using marbles or beads, try doing some addition and subtraction. Here is an example to get you started:

40 + 12 = 52

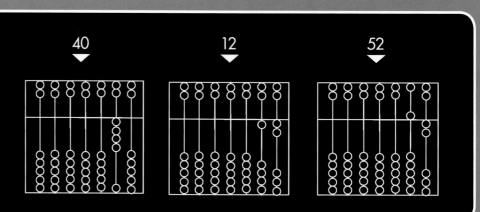

40   12   52

The first calculator was invented in 1642 by mathematician Blaise Pascal. It was designed to help calculate how much tax people owed. By turning linked cogs, it could add and subtract one number from another. It did multiplication and division through repeated addition and subtraction. Sadly the machine was too complicated to be very successful.

TECHNOLOGY TALK

A great step forward in the development of programmable machines was a loom invented by Joseph Marie Jacquard in 1804. Looms are machines that weave cloth. What was extraordinary about Jacquard's loom was that, for the first time, weavers could program the loom to weave a pattern. The program was in the form of punched cards with holes representing the colored threads making each pattern.

COMPUTERS EVERYWHERE

WHEN YOU THINK OF A COMPUTER, YOU PROBABLY IMAGINE A MACHINE WITH A SCREEN AND A KEYBOARD. THESE ARE CALLED PERSONAL COMPUTERS (PCS) BECAUSE THEY ARE FOR GENERAL USE BY PEOPLE. BUT SOME COMPUTERS LOOK QUITE DIFFERENT.

There are several types of personal computers:

DESKTOP COMPUTERS These heavy computers are kept in one location. They have a separate screen and keyboard and use a mouse to point at different locations on the screen. Most desktop computers also have a speaker, microphone, and webcam.

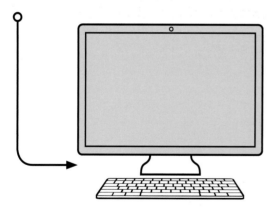

LAPTOPS These lightweight computers are usually in a "clamshell" form with a keyboard in the lower part of the "shell" and a screen in the upper part. Their pointing device is operated by using a touchpad or trackpad.

SMARTPHONES In addition to making voice calls and sending text messages, these mobile phones offer some of the same features as personal computers. They can access the Internet and run software.

TABLETS Tablets are flat, handheld devices. They are operated by touching the screen, which is called a touchscreen. Tablets have a camera, speaker, and microphone, as well as an "accelerometer," which monitors movement and makes sure the display screen is always upright.

There are "hidden" computers everywhere. These computers are often programmed to perform a more limited set of tasks than personal computers. Most of them do not have a screen, keyboard, or mouse, so you probably do not recognize them as computers at all. But there are computers inside machines as varied as game consoles, cameras, cars, airplanes, traffic lights, and robotic toys.

Just like your personal computer, the computer inside a cash machine works with data. That data includes your secret personal number (PIN), the amount of cash you want to withdraw, and the total amount of money you have in your bank account. The computer's software gives instructions on how to use that data and how to display the results of the work, which is usually by giving out cash.

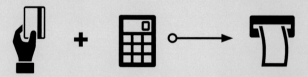

PROJECT

What tasks can you carry out on a personal computer? With an adult's help, use a computer to perform these tasks over the next week. In each case, write down the name of the software you used to do it.

- Write a story.
- Draw a picture.
- Access a kid-friendly website.
- Play a song.
- Create a presentation to display the results of your software research.

ONES AND ZEROS

A COMPUTER'S **ELECTRICAL CIRCUITS** CANNOT STORE AND PROCESS DATA IN THE FORM OF WORDS OR PICTURES. COMPUTERS TURN ALL THE DATA THEY RECEIVE INTO A FORM THEY CAN WORK WITH QUICKLY—NUMBERS.

Computers are **digital** devices. This means that they carry out all their operations using digits (numbers). Computers actually only work with two numbers—0 and 1. These are known as **binary** numbers.

" MATH TALK

In the binary number system, there are no numbers 2, 3, 4, 5, 6, 7, 8, and 9. Despite this, any number can be given in binary form. In binary form, counting starts like this:

Binary Value	Decimal Value
0	0
1	1
1 0	2
1 1	3
1 0 0	4
1 0 1	5
1 1 0	6
1 1 1	7
1 0 0 0	8
1 0 0 1	9
1 0 1 0	10

Can you see the pattern? Now try counting from 11 to 20.

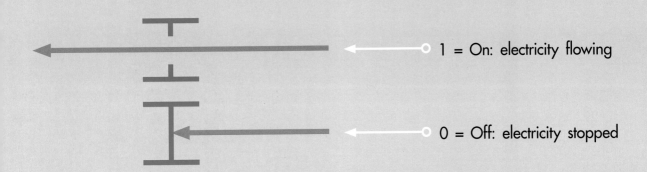

1 = On: electricity flowing

0 = Off: electricity stopped

Binary numbers turn a computer's electrical circuits on and off. The CPU contains many tiny circuits with switches in them. Like a light switch, these mini switches turn the flow of electricity in the circuit on or off. A 1 turns the electricity on. A 0 turns it off. The constant turning on and off of electrical circuits is what allows a computer to carry out its work.

TECHNOLOGY TALK

The tiny switches in a computer's electrical circuits are called **transistors**. They are made of a material called silicon, which can be treated with chemicals to either let electricity flow or stop it. Switches are made from silicon treated in both ways. John Bardeen, William Shockley, and Walter Brattain invented transistors in 1947. Since then, transistors have gotten smaller and smaller. Today they can be as tiny as a nanometers. A nanometer is a millionth of a millimeter.

This is a **circuit board**, which is a board with electrical circuits mapped out on it. The silver-colored plugs are large, old-fashioned transistors. Today's transistors are so small they can be seen only under a microscope.

A COMPUTER'S BRAIN

THE CENTRAL PROCESSING UNIT OR CPU IS A KEY PIECE OF HARDWARE. IT CARRIES OUT ALL A COMPUTER'S CALCULATIONS AND CONTROLS ITS OTHER HARDWARE.

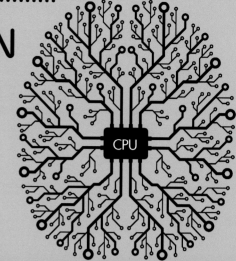

CPU

To carry out any task, every computer follows the same process:

INPUT The computer receives data. This is known as input.

MEMORY When a computer receives input, the CPU and the memory work hand in hand. The CPU reads programs stored in the memory, and it also stores data in the memory.

PROCESSING The computer processes the data in its CPU.

OUTPUT The computer gives the user the results of its work. This is known as output.

THINKING OUTSIDE THE BOX!

You can think of your brain as your own CPU. Consider how you do a calculation:

1 You receive the instruction from your teacher to add 1 + 2.

2 You search your memory for the method of how to do addition.

3 You use your brain to figure out the sum.

4 You give your result (which is 3) by writing it down or telling your teacher.

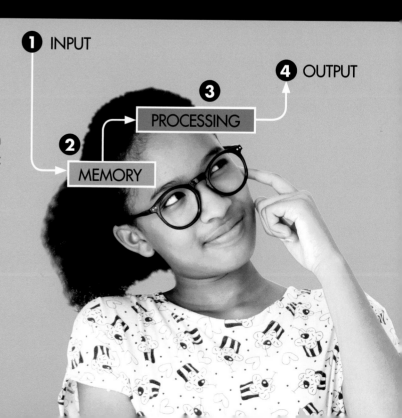

1 INPUT

2 MEMORY

3 PROCESSING

4 OUTPUT

Modern CPUs are small, flat "chips" of silicon called **microprocessors**. Microprocessors contain billions of tiny circuits with switches that can be turned on or off. Before microprocessors were invented in 1971, computers were very bulky because they were built from racks of **circuit boards** containing many different circuits (see page 23).

MATH TALK

The more switches, or transistors, a CPU has, the faster it can process data. In 1975 electronics expert Gordon Moore predicted that computer processing power would double every two years. He was right! That's because we have learned how to make transistors tinier and tinier and pack them onto microprocessors. Currently the most powerful microprocessor contains more than 19 billion transistors. However, will the increase in processing power continue? Some people think that transistors are now as small as they possibly can be.

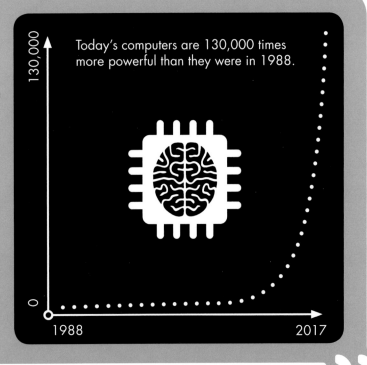

Today's computers are 130,000 times more powerful than they were in 1988.

130,000

1988   2017

MEMORY

TWO IMPORTANT PARTS OF A COMPUTER'S MEMORY ARE FOUND ON ITS MOTHERBOARD— THE ROM AND THE RAM. A USER CAN ALSO SAVE INFORMATION TO A COMPUTER'S HARD DISK OR BY PLUGGING IN AN EXTERNAL MEMORY DEVICE.

Hard disks save data onto a spinning disk within a computer. When the data is needed again, the moving arm goes straight to the correct area of the disk.

ROM
The "read-only memory" stores programs and data even when the computer is off. The computer's user cannot save anything to the ROM.

RAM
The "random access memory" is where data is stored while the user is working. When the user turns off the computer, the data will be lost unless it is saved to the hard disk first.

HARD DISK
Hard disks are found in desktop computers, while some tablets use memory chips instead. The hard disk is where the user can store programs and **files**. Files are blocks of data, such as a letter or a photo.

" MATH TALK

In 1956 the first hard disk weighed 2,200 pounds (1,000 kg) and was bigger than a refrigerator. It stored only 5 megabytes of data. Today's most powerful hard disks are just 2.5 inches wide and hold 60 terabytes of data (see Math Talk on page 15).

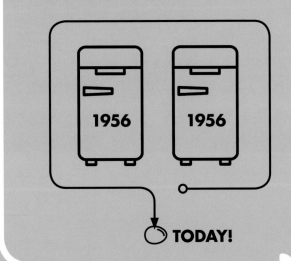

1956   1956

TODAY! "

If you need more memory space, you can save data onto external memory devices. It is also good practice to back up, or make copies of, files on an external device in case your computer breaks.

MEMORY STICK
Memory sticks (also known as flash drives or USB sticks) can fit into a pocket and are useful for carrying data from one computer to another.

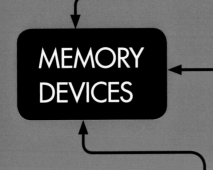

MEMORY DEVICES

MEMORY CARD
Memory cards can be slipped into laptops, tablets, and smartphones.

CLOUD STORAGE
Cloud storage is when data is sent over the Internet and saved onto computers somewhere else in the world, usually in a **data center**. (See pages 32–33.)

" MATH TALK

Like distance is measured in inches, feet, and miles, memory is measured in bytes, kilobytes, megabytes, gigabytes, and terabytes. One byte holds 8 binary digits (bits). A kilobyte holds 8,000 binary digits. A terabyte holds 8 trillion binary digits. A file containing 1,000 letters or characters of text equals 1 kilobyte, while a photo taken by a digital camera is 1 megabyte or more.

→ INPUTS

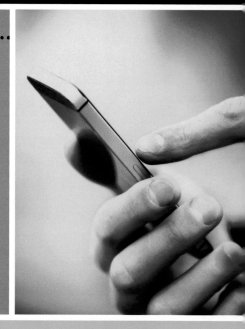

YOU ARE PROBABLY FAMILIAR WITH USING INPUT DEVICES SUCH AS A KEYBOARD, MOUSE, AND TOUCHSCREEN. THERE ARE ALSO MANY OTHER DEVICES AND **SENSORS** THAT CAN GIVE A COMPUTER INFORMATION.

KEYBOARDS On a computer keyboard, each key is a switch that sends an electronic signal to the computer. The computer's software is able to interpret the different key presses.

SCANNERS Scanners are used to capture images of photos or paper documents placed in the machine. A color scanner registers how much red, green, and blue are in each tiny portion of the image. The scanner then converts this information into digital form.

MOUSE Usually a mouse shines a bright light onto your desk, some of which reflects back off the desk into a sensor. As the mouse moves, the pattern of reflected light changes. The mouse converts these patterns into electronic signals.

BARCODE READERS These input devices read the barcodes that label goods. Barcodes are patterns of black and white lines that represent numbers. A light sensor shines a beam of light onto the barcode and measures the reflected light. Black reflects less light than white. The reader translates the pattern into binary digits— black is 1 and white is 0.

0 10421 25071 3

THINKING OUTSIDE THE BOX!

Computer mice do their job so well that most people never think about alternatives. However, there are other handheld pointing devices that are not as widely used. One is a stylus, which is a pen-shaped device that can be used with touchscreens. Another is a light pen, which shines light onto a special computer screen. Can you think of a new design for a handheld input?

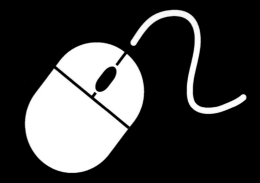

Some computers accept inputs that are spoken. To accept voice inputs, a computer needs a microphone and speech recognition software. When we speak, our words have patterns of loud and soft sounds. For example, a hard consonant, like a K, is a sudden, loud sound. Voice recognition software compares the patterns of loud and soft with the 46 or so phonemes (speech sounds) in its **database**.

TECHNOLOGY TALK

In place of a mouse, smartphones and tablets have touchscreens, while laptops have trackpads. A grid of electrical circuits lies underneath the touchscreen or trackpad. These pick up the movement of your fingers and send electrical signals to the computer. Many touchscreens can recognize particular touches, such as pinches to zoom in and swipes to turn the pages of an ebook.

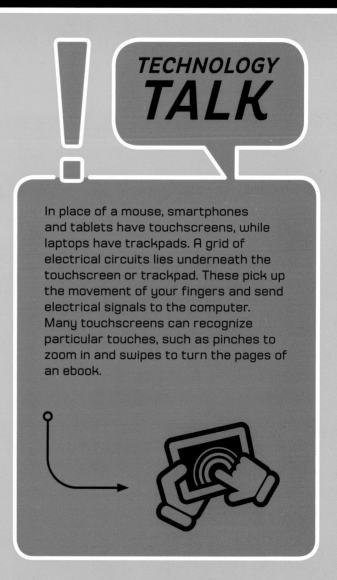

OUTPUTS

WHEN YOU TYPE WORDS INTO A COMPUTER, THE COMPUTER USUALLY SHOWS THEM ON ITS SCREEN. IT CAN ALSO SEND THEM TO A PRINTER, OR IT CAN BROADCAST THEM THROUGH A SPEAKER. THESE ARE ALL OUTPUT DEVICES.

Today computer screens are usually liquid crystal displays (LCDs). LCDs are covered in thousands of **pixels**, or tiny areas of the screen. Each pixel has three subpixels—red, green, and blue. When an electronic signal containing data (such as words, a picture, or a video) is sent to a pixel, the liquid crystal changes to allow light to shine through. Depending on the color the pixel needs to show, it allows light to shine through the red, green, and blue subpixels in different amounts. Any color can be created by combining those three colors.

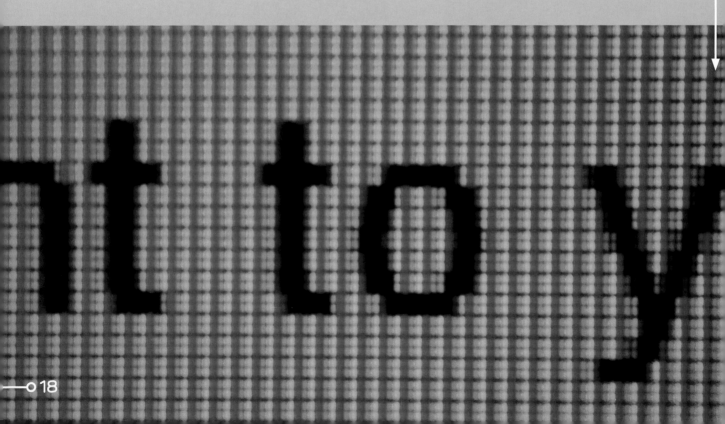

THINKING OUTSIDE THE BOX!

If you look back at the "hidden" computers on page 9, you might be able to think of more output devices for computers. For example, the computer inside a traffic light is programmed to change the color displayed by its lights in a sequence. The lights are its output device. What do you think are the output devices for a talking robot?

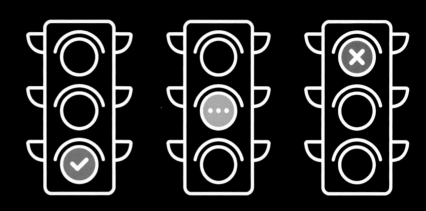

A computer sends data to a printer as electrical signals through wires, or as radio waves through the air. The printer converts the signals into their final form—a black-and-white document, a color photo, or even a three-dimensional (3D) object. 3D printers create an object layer by layer, using plastic or metal.

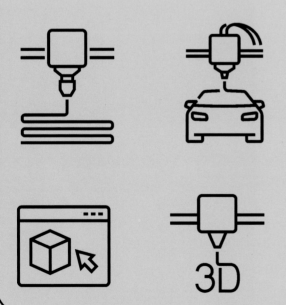

TECHNOLOGY TALK

Another common computer output is sound, such as speech, sound effects, or music. Sound travels through the air as vibrations. These vibrations are picked up by a computer's microphone, which turns them into electrical signals. A computer's sound card converts these signals into binary numbers. Many computer programs can be used to edit sounds. To output, the sounds are turned back into electrical signals and sent to a computer's speaker. The signals make the speaker's cone vibrate, creating sounds.

PROGRAMMING

A PROGRAM IS AN ORDERED SET OF INSTRUCTIONS. COMPUTER PROGRAMMERS WRITE THEIR INSTRUCTIONS IN ONE OF MANY PROGRAMMING LANGUAGES, WHICH ARE OFTEN CALLED CODES.

First, programmers decide exactly what they want the computer to do. Then they break down the instructions into step-by-step commands that cannot be misunderstood. Rather than typing the same command over and over, programmers often create subroutines. These are parts of a program that need to be repeated. For example, every time the programmer wants to command the computer to play a tune, they tell the computer to run the "play a tune" subroutine. Sometimes even experienced programmers make mistakes, though. A bug is any mistake that stops a program from working, like saying "Turn left" when you mean "Turn right."

PROJECT

Write a program that commands a friend to walk around the playground.

- Choose a pattern for your friend to walk in, perhaps a square or triangle shape.

- Break down your instructions into easy-to-understand commands, such as number of steps forward and quarter or half turns.

- Do you want to include any subroutines?

- Now insert a bug into your program, but don't cause your friend an injury!

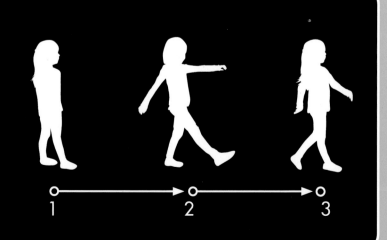

1   2   3

COMPUTER PROGRAMS.

Different programming codes or languages are written in collections of numbers, symbols, or words. Whatever the programming language, a computer's "interpreter" program converts it into strings of 1s and 0s. The computer languages you might use in school include Scratch, Logo, Java, and Python.

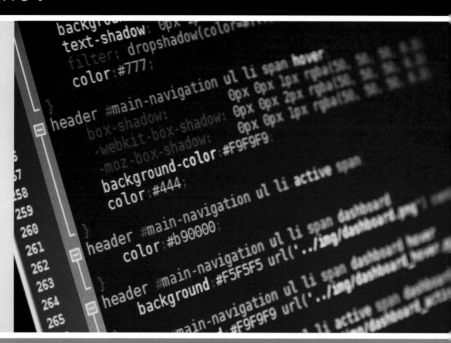

PROJECT

With an adult's permission, try out Scratch. With Scratch it is easy to program a character, or sprite, to move around the screen. A sprite does what you say, like your friend on the playground. The standard Scratch sprite is a cat. You give it instructions in the form of colored blocks with commands written on them, such as "Move 10 steps."

- Go to https://scratch.mit.edu/ and click "Try It Out."
- Find the blocks that command the cat sprite to move. They are in the dark blue Motion group in the center of the screen. Drag some of those blocks over to the empty area on the right side of the screen.
- Click on the blocks to see what the sprite does.

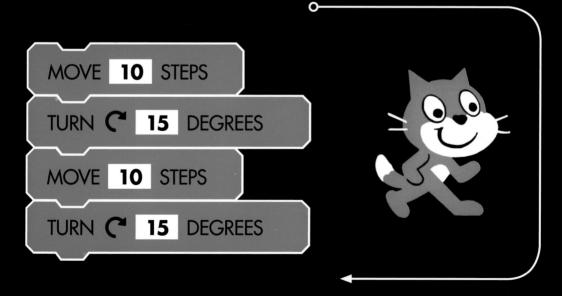

HALL OF FAME: COMPUTER SCIENTISTS

THE TECHNOLOGY IN YOUR LAPTOP OR SMARTPHONE WAS DEVELOPED STEP-BY-STEP OVER MANY DECADES. SOME GREAT THINKERS AND INVENTORS PLAYED A ROLE IN THAT JOURNEY.

CHARLES BABBAGE (1791–1871)

English mathematician Charles Babbage is often called the "father of computing." In 1837 he designed what would have been the first programmable computer, the Analytical Engine, but he never finished it. Babbage designed it to be a calculating machine that used punched cards like those invented by Joseph Marie Jacquard (see page 7). Any calculation could be carried out by a system of interlocking gears. The machine was to be powered by steam.

ADA LOVELACE (1815–1852)

Ada Lovelace, daughter of the English poet Lord Byron, was a friend of Babbage's. A talented mathematician, she believed the Analytical Engine could be more than just a calculator. She wrote the first-ever **algorithm** to calculate sums. This made her the world's first computer programmer. Lovelace also predicted that computers would one day play a huge role in our lives.

HERMAN HOLLERITH (1860–1929)

American inventor Herman Hollerith invented the punch-card tabulator, an electrical machine that recorded and sorted information. This was a breakthrough in data processing. The idea was that any piece of information could be recorded by a hole punched in a card. If a particular area on the card represented gender, for example, a hole there could mean "male." The system was initially used for recording population data for the U.S. census.

ALAN TURING (1912–1954)

British mathematician Alan Turing developed many of our ideas about how computers might work. But his 1936 "Turing Machine" was only a very complex idea, not a real machine. Turing studied how a future electronic computer might be controlled by strings of binary numbers. He predicted that computers would one day be able to think like humans, which we call **artificial intelligence**.

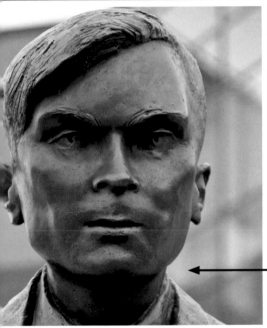

JOHN MAUCHLY (1907–1980) AND J. PRESPER ECKERT (1919–1995)

These American inventors built the first general-purpose electronic digital computer, called ENIAC (Electronic Numerical Integrator and Calculator), in 1946. Its input, output, and memory storage were in the form of punched cards. It could multiply 10-digit numbers 357 times in a second. ENIAC took up 1,800 square feet (167 square meters) of floor space and weighed 30 tons (27 tonnes)!

SOFTWARE

WHEN YOU USE YOUR COMPUTER, ONE TYPE OF SOFTWARE ALLOWS YOU TO DRAW PICTURES, ANOTHER LETS YOU SEND EMAILS, AND ANOTHER LETS YOU SURF THE INTERNET.

A computer's operating system is a key piece of software. It controls the computer's basic functions and how other software uses the CPU and memory. The operating system interprets inputs by turning them into 1s and 0s. Microsoft Windows is the most common operating system for desktop computers. Many mobile devices, such as tablets and smartphones, run the Google Android operating system. Apple desktop computers run the Mac OS operating system, and Apple mobile devices run iOS.

ART TALK

Modern operating systems communicate with the user through a graphical user interface (GUI). They were first developed in the 1970s. A GUI is the system of drop-down menus, docks, and icons that you click on to tell the computer to perform different tasks. We tend to take GUIs for granted, but look more closely to see how cleverly designed they are. Many functions are shown in pictures rather than words. Today children learn to use and understand GUIs in much the same way they learn to read.

Examine the GUI on your personal computer. Would you change its design if you could, or does it already work perfectly?

HOUSEHOLD SOFTWARE

The software on your home computer may include a word-processing program for typing documents, an email program, a browser for viewing websites, and a media player for playing music and videos. Antivirus software prevents your computer from being damaged by dangerous software, called viruses, that travel from computer to computer over the Internet.

PROFESSIONAL SOFTWARE

Many programs were created to help people perform their jobs more easily. These include programs for creating presentations or spreadsheets, design programs in 2D or 3D, website design programs, and programs for creating **animations**.

TECHNOLOGY TALK

Software is designed for a particular purpose and a particular "platform," meaning the type of computer or operating system. For example, some software is designed specially for mobile devices such as smartphones and tablets. These programs are called apps, short for applications. The first app store opened in 2008. Some highly popular game apps have been downloaded more than 500 million times.

GRAPHICS

THE EARLIEST PERSONAL COMPUTERS COULD DISPLAY TEXT AND NUMBERS IN ONLY ONE COLOR. SINCE THEN, DEVELOPMENTS IN COMPUTERS HAVE LED TO MORE REALISTIC AND EXCITING GRAPHICS.

In this 1980s bitmap graphic, it is possible to see the separate pixels.

By the 1980s personal computers began having full-color screens. Beginning in the 1990s, faster processing speeds were making graphics quicker to create. Along with these developments came changes in photography, with photos stored on computers rather than film. Today there are many programs for creating graphics and editing photos. There are two main types of graphics—bitmap and vector.

BITMAP GRAPHICS Pictures are made up of pixels of different colors. Photographs taken on a digital camera as well as many realistic-looking images are bitmaps.

VECTOR GRAPHICS Pictures are made up of lines and shapes. Vectors can be enlarged without the separate pixels becoming visible. **Logos** are often created using vector graphics.

PROJECT

Try out a bitmap graphics program. If you're using a Windows desktop computer, try the free program Microsoft Paint. On a Mac, try Paint X Lite.

- Create a pattern using squares and circles of different sizes. To do this, you will need to find the "rectangle" and "ellipse" tools.
- Find the "fill" tool, then fill the shapes with different colors by clicking inside them. Now print out your design.

RECTANGLE TOOL   ELLIPSE TOOL   FILL TOOL

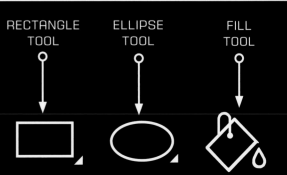

The term computer-generated imagery (CGI) is used to describe the 3D graphics created for video games, films, and TV shows. Outside the world of entertainment, CGI is also used by architects and engineers to design structures. To create a CGI character or building, the artist builds it from a mesh of lines. Then a surface, color, and texture are added to the mesh. Finally, the character or building can be changed and seen from different angles without redrawing it. CGI is created using a combination of bitmaps and vectors.

CGI can make extinct creatures, giant armies, and alien planets look real!

THINKING OUTSIDE THE BOX!

In the early 1990s animators at the Pixar company wanted to make a film using only CGI, which had never been done before. At the time, CGI was not advanced enough to show the range of facial expressions and movements that make people appear human. To solve the problem, the filmmakers made a children's movie with toys as the characters. The result was *Toy Story*, which was released in 1995.

GAMES

COMPUTER GAMES HAVE BECOME INCREASINGLY LIFELIKE, WITH FAST-MOVING GRAPHICS AND REALISTIC SOUND EFFECTS. GAMES CAN BE PLAYED ON A RANGE OF PLATFORMS, FROM GAMING CONSOLES TO SMARTPHONES.

Computer games first became popular in the 1970s. They were usually played on coin-operated machines in arcades. An arcade machine has a video game computer, a screen, speakers, and a game controller in the form of a **joystick**, wheel, or buttons. A game console is a computer specially made for playing games. They can be handheld devices with built-in screens. Home video game consoles are larger and are usually connected to a television screen. Although consoles first appeared in 1967, it was at least another decade before they were widely used. The handheld Game Boy®, which was released in 1989, was one of the first popular consoles.

Across the world, the video game industry makes around $90 billion every year. Games bought for playing on personal computers earn about a quarter of the money. Games played on smartphones make more than $40 million every year, and they are getting more and more popular.

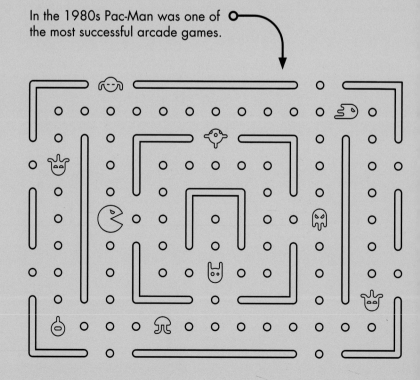

In the 1980s Pac-Man was one of the most successful arcade games.

Most home gaming consoles have handheld controllers as input devices. These use buttons or joysticks for controlling movement in the game. Some game controllers, such as the Wii remote, contain motion sensors. Another common input device is a touch-sensitive mat for use in dancing games. With some consoles, the player does not have to touch an input device at all. For example, the Xbox 360 uses a Kinect camera to detect the player's movements.

The Kinect input device responds to motion and spoken commands.

ART TALK

Many popular games offer virtual worlds where players can interact with other players. The player chooses an **avatar**, a character that represents them in the world. Often the avatar can be designed by the player to look like them or to be strange and surprising. In an ordinary game, the graphic backgrounds may be realistic or beautiful, but in a virtual world they are designed as a key part of the player's enjoyment and interaction with the game. Popular virtual worlds include Minecraft and Second Life.

In Minecraft players can design their own houses, parks, and cities.

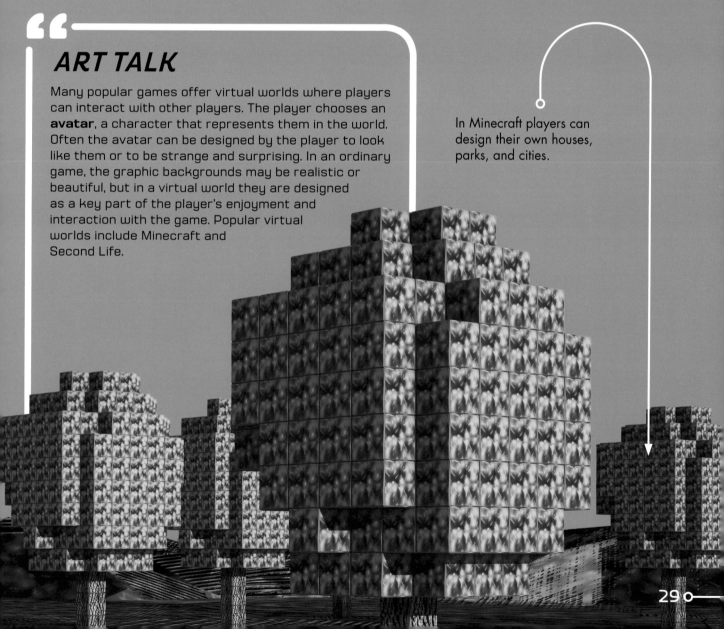

THE EARLIEST COMPUTERS FILLED A WHOLE ROOM. AS A RESULT, THEY COULD BE USED ONLY BY GOVERNMENTS AND LARGE ORGANIZATIONS. A SERIES OF BREAKTHROUGHS LED TO THE DEVELOPMENT OF TODAY'S PERSONAL COMPUTERS, WHICH ARE FOUND IN OFFICES, HOMES, AND POCKETS.

APPLE II, 1977

This was one of the first ready-to-use personal computers with a microprocessor. It was designed by Steve Jobs and Steve Wozniak, the cofounders of the Apple computer company. The Apple II was initially sold for $1,298, which would be about $5,000 today.

MOUSE, 1964

The mouse was invented by American computer engineers Douglas Engelbart and William English. The first mouse had a wooden shell, a circuit board, and two metal wheels. Eight years later, English replaced the wheels with a ball that could monitor movement in any direction. In 1973 the Xerox Alto was the first desktop computer to be used with a mouse.

SMARTPHONE, 1992

In 1992 the IBM Simon was the first mobile phone to run software. It also had a touchscreen that used a stylus. Applications included an address book, calendar, calculator, clock, and electronic notepad. Simon could also send and receive emails. In 1997 the first smartphones were given web browsers for searching the Internet.

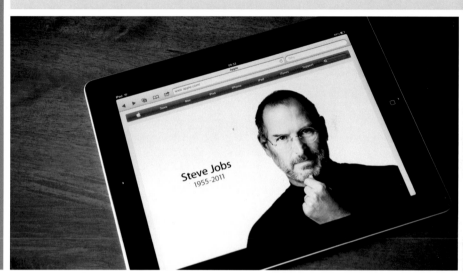

IPAD, 2010

Tablet-style computers have been available since the early years of the 21st century, but they did not become truly popular until Apple launched the iPad in 2010. The iPad's success is due to its many built-in functions, such as a **wireless** Internet connection, camera, and music library.

GOOGLE GLASS, 2013

This wearable computer features a screen and camera. It accepts inputs from voice commands and a touchpad on the side. Google Glass has its critics, but it also has uses in the medical field, for athletes, and the military.

NETWORKS

THE EARLIEST NETWORKS USED WIRES TO CONNECT THE COMPUTERS IN A BUILDING. TODAY THE INTERNET IS A VAST COMPUTER NETWORK COVERING THE ENTIRE WORLD.

Networks are a way of sharing data and other resources. Wired networks are created by copper wires or optical fibers. Some homes are connected by copper wires, along which data is sent as electrical signals. Most new networks use optical fibers, along which data travels as pulses of light. Optical fiber networks carry data much faster than copper wires.

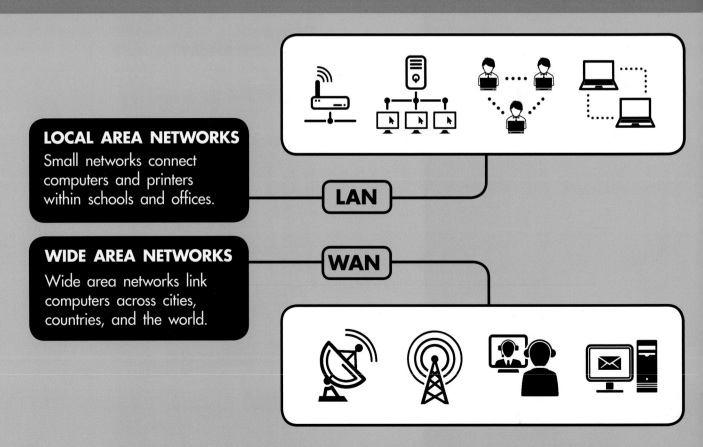

LOCAL AREA NETWORKS
Small networks connect computers and printers within schools and offices.

LAN

WIDE AREA NETWORKS
Wide area networks link computers across cities, countries, and the world.

WAN

TECHNOLOGY
TALK

In a wireless network, data is usually sent and received using radio waves. On a global scale, communications satellites orbiting Earth receive and transmit data wirelessly. On a smaller scale, wireless local area networks often use a system called Wi-Fi. A Wi-Fi network covers a single home or business. A device called a wireless router sends and receives radio waves within the building. The router is often connected to a larger network, either wired or wireless.

People often use the words *web* and *Internet* as if they mean the same thing. But the Internet is a worldwide network made up of thousands of miles of cables as well as wireless connections. Like all networks, the Internet is a way of exchanging data. It is commonly used for sending and receiving emails. It is also used for accessing millions of websites, also known as the web.

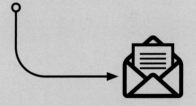

MATH TALK

In 1969 what would later become the Internet as we know it was developed. It connected UCLA and the Stanford Research Institute in California. At first, there were just a few people connected to the Internet. Today more than 3.7 billion people are connected to it.

• Iceland has the highest percentage of Internet users, with 98 percent of its population having Internet access.

• Eritrea in East Africa has the lowest percentage of Internet users. Less than 1 percent of Eritrea's citizens have Internet access.

Internet Users in the World

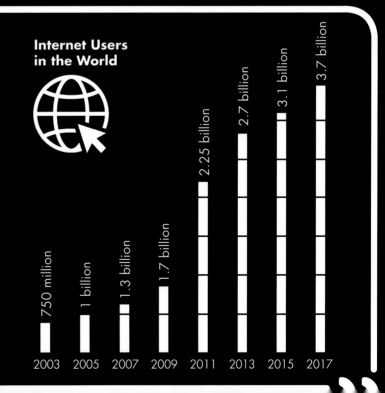

2003	2005	2007	2009	2011	2013	2015	2017
750 million	1 billion	1.3 billion	1.7 billion	2.25 billion	2.7 billion	3.1 billion	3.7 billion

THE WEB

WHENEVER WE LOOK AT A WEBSITE, WE ARE USING THE WORLD WIDE WEB. WEBSITES ALLOW US TO FIND OUT THE NEWS, WATCH VIDEOS, BUY CLOTHES, PLAY GAMES, AND CHAT WITH FRIENDS.

A website is a document stored on a computer somewhere in the world. These documents can contain words, images, and videos. Websites are written in a special computer language called Hypertext Markup Language (HTML). Websites and web pages are connected by hyperlinks. When we click on a link, we move from one web page to another.

The web was invented in 1989 by British computer scientist Tim Berners-Lee.

TECHNOLOGY TALK

We view websites using software called a web browser. Google Chrome and Internet Explorer are popular browsers. When we type the address of a website into our browser, the browser sends a request over the Internet. It asks the computer storing the website to send it to our computer. The data is returned via the Internet. The browser then follows the instructions in the HTML to display the website on our computer. And it all happens in a matter of seconds!

Web addresses are like postal addresses—they are a way of identifying a particular website. All web addresses start with the letters "http", which stands for Hypertext Transport Protocol. This is a set of rules that govern how websites are transported over the Internet. Most websites then have the letters "www", which stand for World Wide Web. The end of a web address, called its suffix, can tell us something about the organization that runs the website, for example:

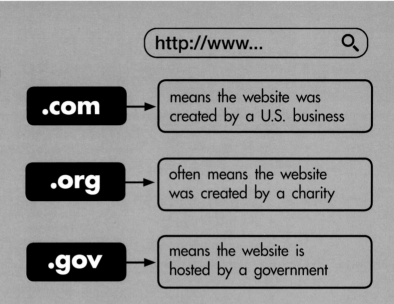

.com → means the website was created by a U.S. business

.org → often means the website was created by a charity

.gov → means the website is hosted by a government

THINKING OUTSIDE THE BOX!

The World Wide Web opens up huge possibilities for knowledge and communication. However, when we are using the web, it is important to think about how we do it. Anyone can create a website containing information that is false or harmful. When we use websites that allow us to communicate directly with other people, often called **social networking**, we need to think about how we behave and watch out for how others behave. Since the web is created by people, it can only be as good or as bad as the people who use it.

VIRTUAL REALITY

VIRTUAL MEANS ALMOST. VIRTUAL REALITY IS WHEN A COMPUTER CREATES A WORLD THAT APPEARS TO BE RIGHT IN FRONT OF YOU, BUT IT'S REALLY ONLY THE PRODUCT OF A PROGRAM.

Rather than viewing virtual reality on a screen, it is viewed through a headset. In gaming, virtual reality headsets allow players to feel as if they are completely in the world of the game. Motion sensors in the headset pick up on head movements. The program then changes the view to match these movements. Virtual reality gloves and bodysuits give the feeling of touching something in the virtual world by applying slight pressure to the skin.

"ART TALK

Augmented reality (AR) can be found in software for mobile computer devices, such as smartphones and tablets. Augmented reality is different from virtual reality. It offers a view of the real world through the device's camera with added features, such as useful or entertaining graphics, sounds, or text. The game Pokémon Go, which was released in 2016, features virtual creatures who appear on-screen as if in the real world. Players must locate them. A drawback of augmented reality is that users can be distracted from being careful in the real world. In 2016 two men playing Pokémon Go walked off a cliff! Luckily they were not badly hurt."

Although virtual reality is most commonly used in games, it is also used in some workplaces. Its technology can be helpful for training soldiers. It helps them experience the feeling of being in battle without putting them at risk. Surgeons are also able to train using virtual reality, giving them a lifelike experience of performing surgery without the need for a human body.

This soldier is learning how to make a parachute jump using virtual reality.

THINKING OUTSIDE THE BOX!

Can you think of other jobs or activities for which virtual reality would be useful? What about situations where augmented reality could offer helpful features? Consider the worlds of education, construction, shopping, transportation, and government.

ARTIFICIAL INTELLIGENCE

CURRENTLY MOST PERSONAL COMPUTERS ONLY DO EXACTLY WHAT WE TELL THEM TO DO. HOWEVER, SOME COMPUTERS ARE PROGRAMMED TO "THINK FOR THEMSELVES," LIKE HUMANS DO. THESE COMPUTERS ARE SAID TO HAVE ARTIFICIAL INTELLIGENCE.

Computers just do whatever they are told by their programs. AI itself is created by programming. AI programs use mathematical algorithms to allow a computer to decide between different responses to a question. These programs also allow the computer to "learn" from past events. This is also accomplished through algorithms. For example, if action A produces this result, but action B produces a better result, in the future action B will be chosen.

THINKING OUTSIDE THE BOX!

Computers and robots with AI have been featured in fiction since 1921, when Czech writer Karel Capek wrote a play about robots rebelling against their human masters. Countless other books, films, and TV shows have focused on the dangers of computers thinking for themselves, including the 2004 film *I, Robot* and the TV shows *Eve* and *Humans.* Why do you think AI both fascinates and worries humans?

The robot Nao contains a computer that runs AI programs.

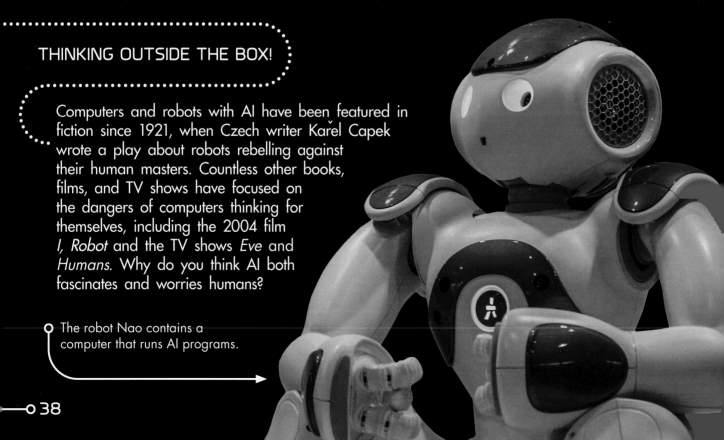

In 1950 Alan Turing (see page 23) developed a test to judge a computer's ability to think like a human. The Turing test has a human tester holding two "conversations"—one with a human and one with a computer. The tester uses a keyboard and screen so he or she cannot see who he or she is talking to. The tester must judge which is the human and which is the computer. In 2014 a computer called Eugene Goostman passed the test for the first time.

In the Turing test, a computer does not have to give correct answers, only the answers that a human would give.

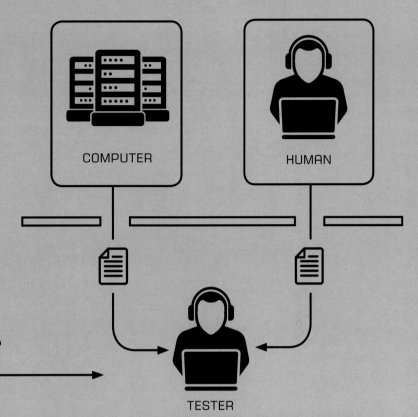

COMPUTER

HUMAN

TESTER

PROJECT

Intelligent personal assistants (IPAs) are programs that perform services for the user, such as answering questions and booking restaurant tables using the web. Most IPAs use speech recognition and AI technology. IPAs decide between a range of answers and seem to get smarter at responding to their users by learning their voice and habits. Some IPAs deliberately choose amusing answers to questions. If you have access to a personal assistant such as Apple's Siri, Amazon's Alexa, or Microsoft's Cortana, carry out your own Turing test.

- How many questions can you ask before the IPA gives an incorrect answer?
- What makes the IPA seem human?
- What makes the IPA seem like a program?

HOW MAY I HELP?

HALL OF FAME: AMAZING COMPUTERS

THESE EXTRAORDINARY COMPUTERS MIGHT CHANGE YOUR IDEAS ABOUT WHAT A COMPUTER IS AND WHAT WORK COMPUTERS CAN DO.

ALMA CORRELATOR

The ALMA correlator is a supercomputer at the ALMA (Atacama Large Millimeter/submillimeter Array) observatory, high in the Andes Mountains in Chile. A supercomputer is a computer with many processors, not just one CPU. The ALMA correlator has 134 million processors and performs 17 quadrillion (that's 17 with 15 zeros!) operations per second. The processors combine and compare radio signals from space, which are received by the observatory's 50 radio antennae. The correlator allows the antennae to work together as a huge telescope, building up images of outer space.

RASPBERRY PI

This computer, which costs less than $35, is used for teaching computing in schools. It is sold as a circuit board containing a CPU and other basic hardware. It can be connected to an electricity supply, keyboard, computer screen, and Wi-Fi networks. The Raspberry Pi has rows of pins into which lights or other devices can be plugged. Students can learn to program the Raspberry Pi to make the lights turn on and off in patterns. Then they can move on to programming robots!

VOYAGER 1

The space probe *Voyager 1* is the farthest man-made object from Earth, which makes its three computers the farthest computers from Earth. *Voyager 1* was launched in 1977 and left the solar system in 2012. The three computers control the probe and its cameras. They receive commands from Earth and send data using the Deep Space Network. This network uses giant Earth-based radio antennae to transmit data.

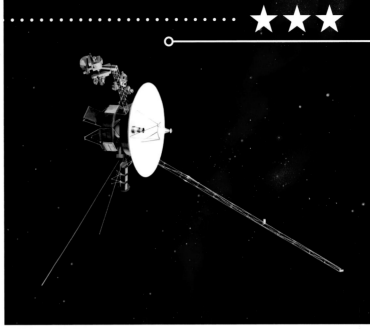

PACEMAKER

A pacemaker is a small electronic device that is placed inside the human chest to monitor and control heart problems. The machine uses electric pulses to keep the heart's muscles working normally. Pacemakers contain a computer, which can be programmed from outside the body by a heart specialist. These computers save hundreds of lives every day.

GOOGLE

Google is not just one computer but a network of around 900,000 powerful computers in Google's data centers. These computers allow the world's estimated 1.17 billion Google users to search the web using the Google **search engine**. Google can be seen as the world's largest computer, or computer cluster. A cluster is a group of connected computers that work together.

A CHANGED PLANET

SINCE THE MIDDLE OF THE 20TH CENTURY, COMPUTERS HAVE CHANGED ALMOST EVERY ASPECT OF OUR LIVES, FROM THE WAY WE WORK AND TRAVEL, TO THE WAY WE HAVE FUN AND TALK TO EACH OTHER.

Before computers became common in offices, many typists and clerks were employed to type letters and documents on mechanical typewriters, or draw graphs and tables with pencils and paper. Before the first robot was put to work in a factory in 1961, factories employed millions of workers for manual tasks. Today there are more than 1.6 million industrial robots. Although many people are glad to do less dull, repetitive work, others ask whether computers will one day put all humans out of work.

THINKING OUTSIDE THE BOX!

Workers no longer have to be in the workplace throughout the day. With email, workers can be anywhere with an Internet connection. Webcams allow meetings to take place without everyone being in the room. "Telepresence" robots take this a step further. Using sensors, microphones, and cameras, a worker who is far away can speak and see through a robot in the workplace, as if they were really there. Telepresence robots are now used in education for giving lessons in remote schools or teaching children who are in the hospital.

The Internet has changed the way we interact with each other. In 2004 Mark Zuckerberg and his friends launched the social networking website Facebook. By 2017 Facebook had 2.2 billion users sharing their opinions, activities, and photos. Today some people may speak face-to-face with just one or two people a day but communicate with hundreds or even thousands online. Although we may feel more connected than ever before, some of us may feel lonelier. Are our online 'friends' real friends? How can we tell if they are who they appear to be?

MATH TALK

In 1950 there were just a handful of computers in the world. Today around 350 million desktop and laptop computers are sold every year. In addition, around 1.5 billion smartphones are sold, as well as 200 million tablets.

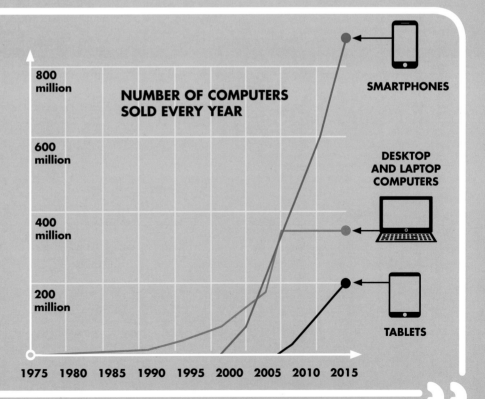

NUMBER OF COMPUTERS SOLD EVERY YEAR

SMARTPHONES

DESKTOP AND LAPTOP COMPUTERS

TABLETS

800 million

600 million

400 million

200 million

1975 1980 1985 1990 1995 2000 2005 2010 2015

FUTURE COMPUTERS

SINCE THE FIRST ELECTRONIC DIGITAL COMPUTERS WERE BUILT IN THE 1940s, COMPUTERS HAVE BECOME MUCH SMALLER AND FASTER. HOW WILL COMPUTERS CHANGE IN THE COMING YEARS?

Computers will probably continue to get faster. However, many people think the current method of computing, which uses electrical circuits in chips of silicon, will have to change to make that happen. Here are some ideas for new computing methods that are in the works:

- **QUANTUM COMPUTERS** could use tiny natural particles to store and process data.
- **CHEMICAL COMPUTERS** could use mixtures of chemicals to perform calculations through their reactions with each other.
- **OPTICAL COMPUTERS** could use lights, which would turn on and off in a way similar to the electric currents in today's computers.

TECHNOLOGY TALK

Some of the devices in our homes hold tiny computers, which communicate with other devices using the Internet. This communication among devices is called the "Internet of Things." These connected devices are referred to as "smart." We already have smart fridges that reorder food and smart heating systems and TVs that can be turned on using smartphones. In the future entire homes may be smart, for example, with bathtubs that run water at bath time.

In the future we may not use real, physical devices, such as laptops or smartphones. Instead, the "devices" we use will be our own digital identity, unique to us, perhaps a name or number. Using that identity, we would access computing systems through non-physical portals (or "doorways") that have yet to be invented. Perhaps data would be viewed using a form of augmented reality.

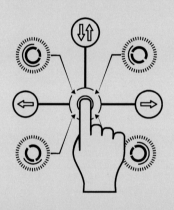

THINKING OUTSIDE THE BOX!

Another possible method of future computing involves integrated nano-electronics. *Integrated* means "linked in" and *nano* means "tiny." This method of computing could work directly from our brain signals, which travel along our nerves as tiny electrical signals. When you wanted to use your computer, which might be worn or implanted in your skin, you would think "switch on" rather than pressing the "on" switch. This sounds like science fiction, but smartphones would have sounded just as far-fetched to someone living in the early 20th century.

GLOSSARY

algorithm (AL-guh-rith-uhm)—a step-by-step procedure for solving a problem, especially by a computer

animations (a-nuh-MAY-shuhnz)—graphics that create the illusion of movement by showing slightly different images one after another

artificial intelligence (ar-ti-FISH-uhl in-TEL-uh-junss)—the ability of a machine to think like a person

avatar (AV-uh-tahr)—a computer icon made to represent a person

binary (BYE-nair-ee)—having two parts; the binary number system uses only the digits 0 and 1

central processing unit (CPU) (SEN-truhl PRAH-ses-ing YOO-nit)—the "brains" of a computer, where most operations are performed

circuit board (SUR-kuht BORD)—a series of circuits that controls many of a computer's functions

data (DAY-tuh)—information stored on a computer

database (DAY-tuh-bays)—a group of computer files that organizes and stores information

data center (DAY-tuh SEN-tur)—a building that holds many networked computers used for storing and processing large amounts of data

digital (DI-juh-tuhl)—using the binary number system to record text, images, or sound in a way that can be used on a computer

electrical circuit (i-LEK-tri-kuhl SUR-kuht)—the path that electricity flows through

file (FYL)—a collection of information stored on a computer

hardware (HARD-wair)—computer equipment that includes internal parts of a computer as well as printers, monitors, or keyboard

input (IN-put)—information fed into a computer

Internet (IN-tur-net)—a computer network that connects millions of computers to each other

joystick (JOI-stik)—a lever that can be moved in several directions and is used to control the movement of an image in a computer game

logo (LOH-goh)—an identifying symbol

microprocessor (my-kro-PROSS-ess-uhr)—a tiny computer processor contained in an electronic computer chip

motherboard (MUHTH-ur-bord)—the main circuit board in a computer that usually holds the main processor and memory

network (NET-wurk)—a system that connects devices to each other

pixel (PIKS-uhl)—one of the tiny dots on a video screen or computer monitor that make up the visual image

processing (PRAH-ses-ing)—operating on data by passing it through a series of actions using a program

radio waves (RAY-dee-oh WAYV)—a form of energy used for sending invisible signals through the air

RAM (RAM)—random access memory; the part of a computer's memory that is lost when the computer is turned off

ROM (RAHM)—read-only memory; memory in a computer with data that can be used but not changed

search engine (SURCH EN-jin)—a program that searches for websites

sensor (SEN-sur)—a device that detects changes, such as heat, light, sound, or motion

social networking (SOH-shuhl NET-wurk-ing)—using computer networks to communicate and form relationships with other people

software (SAWFT-wair)—computer programs

transistor (tran-ZISS-tur)—a small electronic device that controls the flow of electric current

wireless (WIRE-lis)—communicating without connecting wires, usually with radio waves

READ MORE

Bodden, Valerie. *Wearable Technology*. Modern Engineering Marvels. Minneapolis, Minn.: Checkerboard Library, 2018.

Coleman, Miriam. *Designing Computer Programs: Software Engineers*. Engineers Rule! New York: PowerKids Press, 2016.

Spray, Sally. *Computers*. Awesome Engineering. North Mankato, Minn.: Capstone Press, 2018.

INTERNET SITES

Use FactHound to find Internet sites related to this book.

Visit www.facthound.com

Just type in 9781543532296 and go.

 Super-cool stuff! Check out projects, games and lots more at **www.capstonekids.com**

QUIZ

- Write the number 21 as a binary number.

- Who invented the World Wide Web?

- Name an input device and an output device.

- What was the first feature film made completely with computer-generated imagery (CGI)?

INDEX

QUIZ ANSWERS

- 10101
- Tim Berners-Lee
- Input devices include keyboards, mice, touchscreens, and scanners. Output devices include screens, printers, speakers, and lights.
- *Toy Story*